HALLANISH PUBLISHING

This book is a work of recollection. Names, places, characters and incidents are products of the author's memory, and therefore are liable to be wrong, distorted, or seen through rose-colored spectacles. Any resemblance to actual events or locales or persons, living or dead, is entirely on purpose.

48132
Pin - SW

Childhood Memories of Gorebridge
By Ian Hall

4

Hi there.

Here are a few memories from the village I grew up in and its surrounds.

For those many passed away, I remember you with much affection. You know who you are.

For those mentioned by name, I hope they remind you of those seemingly ancient times.

I hope the stories entertain, but I hope also that they bring back memories in your own lives. Maybe you too can put yours to paper, or tell your families.

That's the whole point.

Front Cover
Stobhill Primary School, circa 1968-ish.
Names are in the book at a later chapter.

Back Cover
A Birkenside bus (they pass through Gorebridge), circa 1970. Many a cold stand in Edinburgh or Dalkeith was warmed by the sight of these vehicles.

I wish to thank all of the contributors who have helped with the details or photographs in this work.

Robert Ramsey, Graham & Liz Dixon, Davie Matear, Lynn and James Slight, William Weir, Alex Latto, Valerie Reid, Carol Sheppard and many more who have added their own memories, or perhaps just jogged my memory with a name, a date, or a factoid.

Trust me, without those friendly elbow nudges, this wouldn't have been half as much fun.

Thank you all.
Ian Hall

Introduction

I was born in Edinburgh, in the summer of 1959. Back then most expectant mums in Midlothian were whisked into the city hospital for their childbirth. Mums had little choice in their birthing methods, and like so many thousands, I spent my first days in the Simpson's Royal Maternity Pavilion, Edinburgh Royal Infirmary, Edinburgh.

Seven days later I came home to Gorebridge. Well, to Arniston really, but no one cared much back then. The two villages were stuck to each other like two spots of paint on a wall, kinda smudged at the join. No one really knew where the 'border' was.

My address; 91 Victoria Street (with no post code).

The Hall family, living at 91 Victoria Street, (my first home) around 1915. Ten children were not uncommon at that time. Alexander Mair Hall (My grandfather, Sandy Hall) is far left. My dad remembered his 'Granny Hall' as a scowling, fierce woman; she looks it. In my lifetime I met only three of these people, and was blessed by it.

Unless my parents were writing letters, they never referred to it as Victoria Street. It was always the Tattie Raw. (Potato Row, for the fine diners)

My father (Andrew Hall) had been born there, and his father (Sandy) had lived there for years. Before I could walk or talk, we moved to 103 Victoria Street, the very bottom house on the park side; right at the sand pit.

I have only a few early memories of the house or the park, I remember one bright, sunny day riding in a cab in a tractor in a yellow corn field.

The tractor was definitely red.

I remember cows in that field too, and nervously feeding them grass over the wall (or was it a fence?).

I recall dad digging a lot in the walled garden, and the taste of fresh, green, garden peas straight from the peapod.

(He always complained about kids stealing his peas. It wasn't till years later that my first wife (Elaine Merchant) admitted that she and the kids from the other rows used to rampage our garden. She too, remembered the taste of dad's fresh peas.)

I remember the park, and the steep-walled circular sand pit. Hard concrete steps led down into the beach sand, and I played there for hours.

I don't remember mum looking down on me, watching over her precious child like the mums today.

Dad and me, 103 Victoria Street
(The Tattie Raw) about 1963

Victoria Street is gone now, bulldozed to make way for newer houses, but the park is still there. It's modernized, and all the 'dangerous' rides are gone; the 'Witches Hat' was a crazy helter-skelter roundabout.

The red see-saw, with the horses face, (I somehow remember the name 'Dobbin'), and the imposing, green metal chute. We never called it a slide; it was our 'shoot'.

The 'Monkey Bars'; A huge cubic maze of steel bars, polished to a blue hue by generations of kids climbing them.

And endless 'acres' of thick hedge mazes, and manicured rich green grass.

(There's a chapter on the 'Park', later.)

Around my fifth birthday, we moved up the hill, into the new housing scheme.

56 MacLean Place, but we were definitely over the border into Gorebridge, this time. We had crossed the Auld Arniston Store Rubicon.

And we were important, because we got a letter from the government saying that we now had a postcode; EH23 4DX.

We moved just in time for me to go to Stobhill Primary school, instead of the larger Gorebridge Primary School.

I remember that summer, meeting new friends on all sides; Lynn Slight in 54, and Derek Weir in 58. Christine Nohar across the road in 59. Angela Brownlee across on Wilson Road, and the *'enemies'*; the kids on the 'top road'... the Bartons and Logan's and such.

This bike is the wrong color, but it does show the important bucket.

And driving my sea-green three wheeler bike. Derek had one like it, but his was red, and had no bucket at the back. Mine had a bucket; I could carry stuff, just like Thunderbird Two.

(Don't even get me started on Thunderbirds; the greatest kids TV series, EVER!)

Anyway, I lived at 56 MacLean Place till I was twenty-one, so I got to know the old village very well. Most of the stories are set here. All are true (or as true as I can remember).

Gorebridge and Gunpowder

In the distant past of 1794, Gorebridge held a secret.

It was dark, foreboding secret, but it should be taught to every child in the village in Primary School. Every kid who lives in the so-called sleepy hamlet should know about Gorebridge and the Gunpowder Mill.

(Who knew that when we were conducting our chemistry experiments in our teenage years, that we were duplicating history, rather than rebelling against it.)

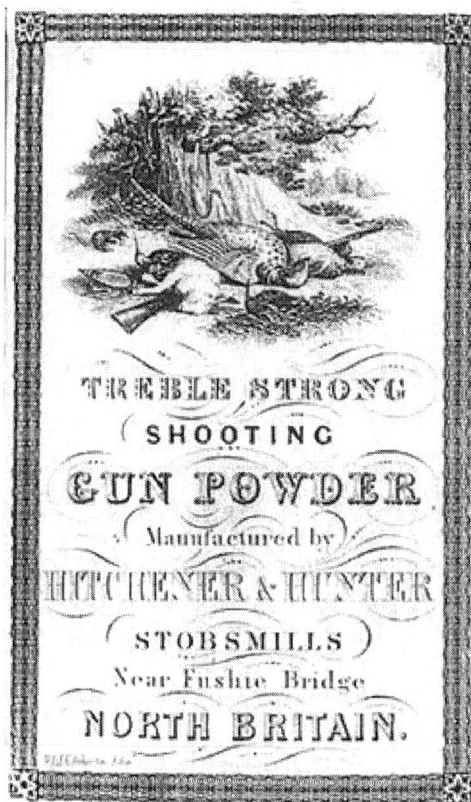

(Look how non-nationalistic the sign is; no mention of Scotland, just North Britain! If you think it through; this was just fifty years after the Bonnie Prince Charlie rebellion, in 1745-6, we Scots were still very much repressed by the English.)

As the advertisement above states, incredibly, Gorebridge was the site of a Gunpowder Mill, actually Scotland's *first* gunpowder factory.

It was under the old Gore Bridge between the Gorebridge High Street and Birkenside.

The ruins of the gunpowder mill are still there on the ground to see, and it has been surveyed as a heritage site. I never knew this history as a child, and feel cheated for it. I would have loved to explore the ruins, just a few hundred yards from Gorebridge Main Street.

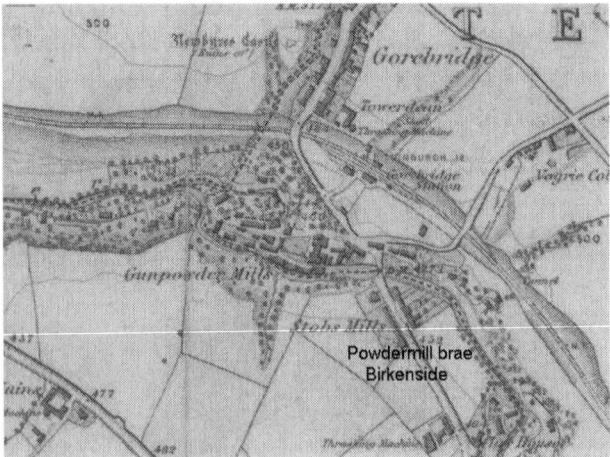

You can see the many buildings on this old map.

An old corn mill was converted, and production of gunpowder at Stobsmills started in 1794. The English investors, William Hitchener and John Hunter, leasing the land from the Buccleuch Estates, worked under the bridge to produce the best quality gunpowder in the country.

The gunpowder mill needed water in the process, so sluices and many dams were built into the Gore water to supply ten water wheels. All in all, over twenty buildings were used in production.

But it was a dangerous occupation, in a time of little or no safety policy, and explosions, injuries and deaths often occurred. Huge explosions in 1825 and 1827 saw death, and damage to the whole village.

Initially, in a time of peace, the mill advertised as a sporting company. But soon, Britain was involved in a struggle against Napoleon Bonaparte, and many cartloads of their black powder product were sent north to Leith docks, then by sea to Grangemouth, then by canal to Greenock, then to Liverpool, to be shipped to the army in Europe.

For the Gorebridge historians, the street name "Powdermill Brae" is a certain clue to this truth of this history. (Powdermill Brae runs uphill from the Gore, (or Fushie) bridge, up past the railway station, to Main Street. A row of cottages (now long gone) in Birkenside were called the "Black Raw" (Black Row), and supposedly the name came from the wives beating the blackened clothes of their husbands against the house walls to dislodge the powder.

There is a tale of a worker who lit his pipe by scratching a match on the wall of his cottage, and the resultant rippled explosion shook the walls.

The mill initially had a fifty year lease on the land, and ceased production around 1861.

I now turn my attention to two newspaper reports of the aforementioned explosions. The language of the day leaves nothing to the imagination.

The 1825 Explosion.

The following news report on the gunpowder explosion of 1825, is taken from a Robert McMillan Broadside, probably printed in Edinburgh.

13

The sheet, priced at just one penny, was single sided, designed to be read unfolded, and sold by peddlers and chapmen.

Following the broadside, is a newspaper report of another explosion in Stobsmills.

In both I have corrected the bad spelling, inserted some extra detail, and adjusted phrases and place names for accuracy.

"Dreadful Explosion.

A Full and Particular Account of that Dreadful Explosion of Gunpowder, at Stobsmills, on Thursday last the 17th February, 1825, at a few minutes past Eight in the morning, by which two Men and a Horse lost their lives, and several others were severely injured.

About ten minutes after eight yesterday morning the inhabitants of the adjacent villages of Stobbs (old name for "stopping place") and Gorebridge, and neighborhood, were thrown into great alarm, in consequence of an explosion of gunpowder, which took place at one of the branches of the extensive manufactory which Messrs. Hitchener and Hunter have for many years carried on at Stobsmills. The accident is one of such a nature as precludes all possibility of ascertaining how it originated, which, of course, must, must ever remain matter of conjecture; all that is known is, that a man named Walter Thomson had gone with a cart loaded with powder from one of the mills to the charge-house, a kind of temporary store house in which the powder is kept, until there is room in the stove or drying house to receive it, and nearly adjoins the later, and this person must have been in the act of unloading the cart at the moment the explosion occurred. Fortunately, however, the sufferers have been few, is it is ascertained that Thomson (the carter) and an old man named Richard Cornwall employed at the stove, were the only individuals who lost their lives; their bodies were blown to atoms, and small portions of them have been picked up, at great distances from each other, and in such a

14

condition as rendered it impossible to distinguish to which of the two they belonged; the head and neck of one was recognized from the neck cloth about it.

The horse was thrown a considerable distance and some of the barrels of powder which had been placed on the cart were blown in the air, and exploded over the heads of the ploughmen in the fields. The materials of the stove house and charge house, which are both raised to the foundation, are lying in all directions, extending to a circumference of at least half a mile, covering the fields like flocks of birds. So great was the concussion that in the villages scarcely a window has escaped its ravages; that of Stobsmills, although nearest the scene of the explosion, has suffered least, but in Gorebridge many houses have not a whole pane left, and the roofs present a most picturesque appearance ; some entirely unroofed on one side, and from most of the others the tiles are moved down so as somewhat to resemble a sieve.

The meeting-house at Gorebridge has not only suffered in glass, but the astragals of several of the windows have gone alone with the more fragile materials: even at the farm house of Newhouses at least three quarters of a mile from the mills, many of the panes were broken and the doors of some of the houses were burst open. We have heard too that the glass in the hot-houses at Vogrie, three miles distant were broken, and part of the ceiling of the house of Fountainhall was thrown down. The concussion was quite terrific in Dalkeith, four miles distant, and affected the buildings so much as to prevent the doors from shutting and in Ormiston, Tranent, and Musselburgh, it was distinctly felt.

Here, in Edinburgh, fully nine miles from the mills, the two explosions were very generally heard, but supposed by many to be blasts in the neighboring quarries, or a salute from a vessel in the Firth.

The quantity of powder supposed to have exploded is calculated at about six tons weight, forty barrels were in the store, forty or fifty in the charge house, and ten on the cart. The two unfortunate men who were killed had both families."

    In Temple Parish Kirk graveyard lie two reminders of the day.
    One gravestone marks the 'body' of Richard Cornwall, erected by his son Thomas. Richard is marked as dying 17th February, 1825. Charles Hitchener, the original Sussex owner of the mill has a memorial in Temple Kirkyard, paid for by his sister in law. The memorial was refused in Dalkeith parish Church cemetery where Hitchener's body lies, on the grounds that he may have had an affair with the sister in law.

    Another explosion happened just two years later. The following is a Glasgow newspapers coverage, quoting the Edinburgh Caledonian Mercury for central details...

    The 1827 explosion.
    "Awful Explosion.
    An account of that dreadful and melancholy accident which happened on Saturday morning last, 29th Sept, 1827, when the Stobbs powder mill, near Edinburgh, blew up with a tremendous explosion, and a number of men who were in the mill, were killed; some of them had their legs torn off, their bellies torn open, and their bodies thrown to a considerable distance. They were all married. The place was one heap of ruins, a number of cottages were unroofed, and everything surrounding it was burnt up.
    Explosion of a Powder mill.
    (From the Edinburgh Caledonian Mercury of October 1st, 1927.)
    The explosion took place on Saturday morning last, about half-past seven o'clock in what is called the Corning Room. How this lamentable accident occurred must ever remain unknown, as the three men who were employed in the premises at the time, no more being present, were killed in the explosion. One of these unfortunate men had his legs

torn from his body, another his belly torn open, and his entrails hanging out; and the third was blown into a water at a considerable distance from the mill, where he was found dead about an hour later. Search was immediately made for the members which were severed from the bodies; but when found, they were so dreadfully scorched, and the bodies were so terribly mutilated, that it was impossible to know to which the different members belonged.

When looking round the scene of this terrible visitation, it seemed as if some destroying angel had been there, doing his work of desolation and death.

The premises wherein the explosion took place were so shaken to the foundation, and lay in one heap of ruins, the surrounding trees were stript of their foliage, and the grass was burnt black and bare. Cottages might be seen in a state of miserable dilapidation, being almost unroofed, with their windows shattered; and, to add to the afflicting character of the scene, from these ruins might be heard for a father and a husband, whom the cruel destiny of this vile hour had, in an instant, torn from their disconsolate family.

The three unfortunate men who fell victims to this melancholy accident were married, and have left widows; one of them with a family of three children; another only a fortnight married, and a third pregnant. The premises, we understand, were insured."

Gorebridge and Gunpowder. Who would have thought it?

Incidentally, Wikipedia sites three other prominent references for our wee sleepy hamlet.

Annette Crosby, the actress who played Victor Meldrew's wife, in the comedy classic "One Foot in the Grave"; was born in Gorebridge.

The "King's Cave", where we adventured as children, down the Gore Glen, is supposedly 'not' a hiding place for Robert the Bruce as he hid from the English armies, but a cattle riever's hideout.

17

And the Rev. David Arnott, my minister at Stobhill church, Gorebridge, in the seventies, (The man who first taught me the bible and its Hebrew references at Bible Class), is now the Moderator of the Church of Scotland.

The Games We Played

I list the following as a nudge to the other kids who might read this....

Tennis in the street with a rope pulled tight for a net.

(We even had ball boys, but no net. Work that one out. We also painted a single capital letter on the strings of our cheap tennis rackets, just like the real tennis players)

Pickies. (Hopscotch) With a Kiwi shoe polish tin filled with dirt or old plastacine.

Chinese Ropes; us guys could never get that right; hundreds of colored elastic bands, joined together into one huge elasticky hoop. Just right for catching the clumsy feet of the boys who tried the complicated moves.

Skipping..... crappy girl game.

Hide and seek. Easy game, but woe betide you if you got caught going 'round the block'.

Cheating; not allowed.

Ten Tin Soldiers; a variation of Hide and seek.

Incidentally, we did the 'tatties' to see who was 'het' (our parochial version of 'it').

We'd stand in a line against the fence, with our fists (potatoes) out in front of us. One kid stood in front, his fists (potatoes) also out in front.

He would hit out hands counting; "One potato, two potato, three potato, four. Five potato, six potato, seven potato, more!" and he'd hit down the eighth fist. We'd carry on till only one was left.

He/she was 'het' ('it').

Where was I? Oh yes, games.

Bools (Marbles) (It was always a good thing if your dad could get you stainless steel ball-bearings from work; mine could. A 'steelie' was worth at least ten glass marbles.)

Sojers; speaks for itself.

Dead Man's Falls. This was fun, usually done, going down a hill for best effect.

We would line up, with one guy well to the front, usually lying down. He would give us the choice of the method of our death.

(This varied from knife throwing, through various bullet types, to bombs and grenades)

You would advance stealthily on his position, then, miming beautifully, he would deliver the killing blow.

In a pre-determined theatrical death, you would die like so many heroes in the war films on TV or cinema.

My favorite was grenade.

You could die any way you liked when someone threw a grenade at you.

A couple of steps… then you see the grenade… you glance to the side to see if there's enough time to run…. there's not…. it detonates, sending you flying through the air… then you roll, dying MUCH better than the crappy actors… I mean, where do they get their ideas from?

Chap Door Run. Not the best move if you lived nearby. It involved knocking on an 'unknown' front door, then running away as fast as your little legs would carry you. The worst words I would ever hear… "Young Hall, your Dad will hear about this!"

Crap.

The Dumbest Shoes

We lived on the side of a hill, about ten miles south of Edinburgh, on the edge of a housing development added on to the village called Gorebridge. I could walk forty yards and be at, what we called, the 'top road'; the limit of the housing. Beyond that, were fields that led to an ancient Roman encampment on the top of the hill. Nothing much was left of the 'Roman camp', of course; just a few ridges and ditches, but to us it was a place to adventure to, and we'd just tell our Mums that we were 'going up the camp'.

My Papa Hall was in the ARP (Air Raid Precautions) in the Second World War, and he'd stood guard on an unexploded German bomb up the camp once. He said that there was a steady flow of curious onlookers before the bomb disposal team arrived.

From the 'top road' you could look over the whole of Midlothian, right down to Edinburgh itself. On a clear day, you could see everything, Edinburgh Castle, Arthur's Seat, Salisbury Crags. You could even see over the Forth Estuary to Fife, and those two little 'nipple-like' hills; the 'Pap's o' Fife'.

The forty yard hill from the end of our street to the 'top road', had narrow pavements down both sides, the opposite pavement was rough, having been crossed with many repairs, but the one nearest my house was smooth. This didn't matter much most of the time, but in winter when it snowed, it mattered a lot.

It was our slide.

We'd watch out our windows as the snow fell, then we'd venture outside when the snow had stopped and we'd gather excitedly on the hill.

For some reason, the mothers seemed to have it in their heads that we didn't get outside to play till the snow had actually stopped. I'm not sure what the reasoning was, but they all did it. Sometimes, one of us would convince our

23

Mums that it had, and usually just one kid allowed outside would break the floodgates. We would grab hats, scarves, and gloves, and run for the pavement up the hill.

There was no leader, no organizer telling us what to do, we'd done it so many times before, and the technique had changed little in hundreds of years.

Sometimes as many as twenty kids would gather, but just the ones from 'our' end of the street. Other groups had their own slides.

We would take runs across the grass at the top, and then launch ourselves down the hill like we were on skateboards, but of course there were no actual boards; they hadn't been invented yet. We just slid down the pavement on our shoes, our arms waving to keep us balanced, and pretty soon we'd come to a halt with a huge pile of snow that we'd bulldozed down the hill.

Before long, we soon knew who had the 'dumbest shoes', as they didn't travel as far down the hill as the other kids.

To have the 'dumbest shoes' had a bit of stigma to it, but it had nothing to do with the intelligence of the footwear; the 'dumbest shoes' were simply the ones with most grip, the new shoes. "New for the winter" mum would say, and you didn't even get to wear them till it was rainy.

I can even remember getting new shoes or boots for winter, and scuffing all the way to school each morning, trying my hardest to wear the grips down ready for snow.

No-one really wanted to have the 'dumbest shoes'.

The first thirty-or-so goes down the hill had two purposes; one was to rid the pavement of the annoying thick layer of snow, dumb shoes didn't matter much then. The second was to press some of the white stuff into the ground and make ice.

Sheet ice.

Ice so slick that you couldn't stand on it, without either falling on your backside or sliding down the hill.

Ice so smooth, that no matter what the grips on your shoes or wellington boots were like, you couldn't deny the lack of friction nor defy the laws of gravity.

Pretty soon most of the pavement was ice.

When the slide got icier, dumb shoes began to matter a lot, as the grips were so rough that they'd gouge out tracks in the packed snow that we liked to call ice, and therefore 'spoil' the slide. The one with the dumbest shoes was sometimes even banned from the slide, but usually we just let it go and try to get in front of him.

Sometimes we'd fall or go too deep or the 'dumb shoes' kid would take a turn and hit pavement again, so we'd take some new snow and repair the slide, rubbing the patch for a while to bring it up to the same standard as the rest of the hill.

We'd take long runs and feel like we were just a blur as we slid past Mrs. Purves' gate, but the best part of all was sliding down the hill and being able to turn the corner at the bottom. Doing the 'curve' meant you were a seasoned slider and the balance needed to make the bend meant that a good few crashes occurred.

Some kids were good 'sliders' and some weren't, and since we had a huge range of ages amongst the kids, it didn't usually matter, but the older kids always seemed to get round the corner. It was almost a rite of passage.

The pavement was only about five feet wide, so there wasn't much room for error in your sliding. If you went to the right, you'd fall off the curb and go speeding and sometimes tumbling onto the snowy road. Not that we were in danger of being hit by a car; we were at the top of the housing estate, and it sometimes took the snow ploughs days to get to us. Dad even missed work sometimes because of the depth of the snow, and we'd dig out his wheels and try and push the car to the edge of the hill, so he could coast down to the main road, half a mile away.

If you went to the left, you hit Mrs. Purves' fence, a rough chain link that had ripped many jackets and trousers. If there were cars parked on the hill, and that wasn't usual because Mrs. Purves didn't have a car, the chain fence was the only way up the slippery slope and we'd pull ourselves determinedly up the hill, our feet sliding on the ice.

When the slide was 'perfect' and we'd got bored with just sliding down, we'd gather at the top and the word 'train' would be mentioned, and we'd cheer "Train, train!", everyone laughing at the idea.

"Who's got the dumbest shoes?" someone would ask, and we'd each examine the grips on our soles, looking for the biggest, roughest tread, but in our hearts we knew who it was. It was usually the kid standing to the side, seemingly still enjoying themselves, but banned from the actual slide.

It was a great moment. The kid with the 'dumbest shoes' turned from pariah to hero in seconds. Although 'dumb shoes' usually gouged up the slide, they also made great brakes, and on a steep iced hill, the train needed brakes until all the carriages were on.

So the kid with the 'dumbest' shoes was pushed to the edge of the slide, and he'd crouch down as low as he could, his feet flat on the ground, leaning forward. We called it 'down on yer hunkers', and we all knew what it meant.

The next kid would go down on his 'hunkers', and shuffle up to the one with the dumbest shoes, and grip his jacket tightly, with both hands, pushing him over the edge and a foot down the slide. The next kid would join at the back and very soon there was a 'train' moving gradually onto the slide, being held back by the brakes on the 'dumbest shoes'.

Before long, and usually before everyone had got on board, the 'dumbest shoes' caved in to the force of gravity and with a roar of alarm and glee the many legged train began its journey down the hill. It gathered pace quickly, and any kids left at the top soon ran and slid down the slide, following or falling, and sometimes they crashed into the back of the train causing mayhem.

Sometimes the train would linger at the top with everyone attached, and slowly we'd shuffle forward until sheer force of momentum carried us downward.

There were trains that slid down the hill gracefully, till the brakes did their job and eased the train to a steady halt.

There were those that just petered to a halt, a clumsy teetering mess.

But there were trains that started perfectly slow, and gathered speed on the ice, and charged at the curve like a speeding train should. Those were the best. Those express trains usually met with a rather messy end.

A pile of grinning, laughing humanity with arms and legs in every direction.

Eventually, when we'd just think we'd have the perfect winter slide, the worst thing in the universe happened; Mrs. Purves' door would open and she'd begin the slow walk through the virgin snow to the pavement. She held a box of Saxo salt in her hand, and despite our moaning's, she'd sprinkle the salt onto the pavement outside her gate.

We knew that our slide was doomed to melt in the crisp winter sunshine.

There were plenty more places to make a slide, but nothing was as good as Mrs. Purves' pavement.

Wellies, Wellington Boots, Galoshes

There was a time for shoes, like sliding, and there was a time for Wellington boots. Some people called them Galoshes, but we knew better. They were named after the big boots that the Duke of Wellington used to wear. Paddington the bear had blue ones, Christopher Robin's were red, I think, but ours were always black.

We called them 'Wellies'.

Or Welly Boots.

Big, knee high, rubber boots.

Shoes were fine for sliding, but if the snow was deep, our mums would never let us out of the house with just shoes on. We'd be sent out in wellies, usually with big thick socks inside. They were great for wading through the snowdrifts.

Looking back, there was no stigma attached to the wellies; we all had them. If the snow happened on a school day, we'd walk to school in them.

Thousands of pairs of wellies would sit wet and drying in our cloakrooms, usually with big pairs of thick woolen socks hanging over the tops. That always made for a curious smell.

When the snow was dry and flaky, they were the best; we never had to worry about cold feet. When the snow got that little bit more moist, the games changed; we had snowball fights, we'd roll it into huge balls for snowmen or barricades, anything really.

The only thing really wrong with wellies was the wide brim. It was so easy to get snow inside. Or get it pushed inside!

Anyway...

Snow never lasted that long, in Gorebridge, then the thaw started, and it was time for a different game.

Wellies kept out the snow, but they were also great in the wet. Icy, slushy puddles were much better to splash through if they were deep, and we'd look everywhere for the biggest and deepest ones.

When we couldn't find any, we'd make our own.

Find a gradual slope in the road, usually near a drain, and build a dam with the snow. Usually it didn't take long to get a puddle six inches or so. Sometimes deeper, depending on the height of the curb.

Of course, we all knew that disaster could strike at any moment. Building our 'dam' on the road made it susceptible to one thing.

Cars.

Some pig would drive too close to the curb, and our dam, and all the slushy water that had collected got splashed everywhere.

We'd look at the oncoming vehicle, and rapidly evacuate the immediate strike zone, and wonder if they would drive through it. Some didn't, some of our dams were big, holding a whole lot of water, and they'd swerve to miss. We cheered.

Others ploughed right through. The resultant splash also got a great cheer, then we ran to the dam to watch the water pour through the breach, exactly like one of the hits in 'Dam busters'. We'd all seen the film many times. There was no point in trying to fix the dam until all the water was out.

Then we'd start again, rising the walls, looking for deeper water to wade in.

When we got home, we put our wellies by the fire, and try our best to get them dried out. Overnight we'd stuff newspapers inside.

No one liked their feet in wet wellies.

Welly boots.

Rubbers

I also remember rubbers.

They were our gym shoes. (Plimsoles) New every year.

Standard issue; black. Soles; rubber, a sort of neutral tan-brown color with a ripple pattern, and a wee square label that you peeled off.

Everyone had the same. It was great.

Slip-ons till you were old enough to tie your own laces, then tied ones.

No brand names.

No designer colors.

And no ridiculous prices.

Mum would take me down to Abie Broons on a Saturday (Because, let's face it, ALL the shops were closed on Sunday) and we'd buy my new gym shoes for the year. And woe betide me if my feet grew too quickly. Because there wouldn't be money for another pair till same time next year.

I remember one year, I got 'issued' with my new rubbers t go out and play.

It was such a great feeling to be outside with other footwear. A trash truck came along the street, and I ran after it.

Now, it stopped, and I got smartly onto the pavement, next to Angela Brownlee's gate; I mean these trucks were huge compared to me.

The truck reversed, and mum couldn't see me for a minute or two.

I was totally unaware of her being frightened as to what had happened to her running son.

Well, the truck drove away, and there was mum, standing on the other side of Wilson Road, scowling at me.

"Get inside!" she railed. "You wait until your father gets home."

All for being a little exuberant.

It wasn't too long before I hit high school, of course, and 'rubbers' just weren't any good there…

You needed training shoes.

And those had to be bought in Edinburgh; after all, you didn't want any old shoes then.

The designer had his insidious horns in, and you were very conscious about what you wore, and what others did too.

Arniston Park

It's difficult to remember a small area of well-maintained park about a hundred yards square as a tourist destination, but back in the day… it was.

Settled between Tattie Raw, the top of the Toll Brae, and a thin woodland walk down to the A9 Galashiels toll road, Arniston Park typified 'being a kid' to me.

The view from the top of the 'chute'. Circa 1970.

For a start, it had swings.

But at its roots, it had much, much more.

For a start, it was cut into small manageable chunks by huge manicured hedges. Great for hiding, hide and seek, and chases. As kids, we'd crawl thru the holes at the bottom of the privet bushes, and be in a totally different world.

And the grass… always cut to perfection, always neat, never too long.

And there were tar macadam paths. Paths you could ride your three wheeler on until you had exerted every ounce of energy you had.

There was the huge deep concrete built sand pit by the bottom gate.

The Skating Rink. Next to the farmers field at the bottom.

The big brick-built shed, with a huge concrete floor, with bench seats for six hundred (perhaps I exaggerate). We'd sit there in the rain, and tell stories, or just shout up into the rafters and hear it echo.

The see-saw horse. Red. Dobbin. If you could get it going, it'd bang at each end of its arc.

Not 'our' Dobbin, but you get the idea.

The Witches Hat. Dark Green, with a red top, if I remember right. Okay, it was a very primitive kind of framework, but if we all stood on the seats ("beaming", Frances Forrester remembers) we'd get the whole thing rocking violently, and each upwards spar would jar against the top, vibrating so much, we thought we'd soon break it.

Again, not our hat, but this gives you an idea.

The Monkey Bars. Great for climbing, great for the younger kids to walk around the bottom, avoiding being kicked by the other climbing kids. These steel bars had rust in the corners, but the middle of the spars were polished to a blue shine by the hands, feet, and clothes of a generation.

The Monkey Bars. Never-ending fun.

Swings. Yeah.

The Roundabout. Again, dark green.

The Chute at the top (main) gate. Dark green. Oh boy, it was high. And bringing our mums old plain bread wrapper to shine it with. On a good day, you'd go shooting down the slope, flying right along the flat bit, and land on the concrete with a loud yelp. Just like on snow slides, we'd also do trains; clinging to each other like glue until we couldn't hold on any more. I don't know how we survived those wild carefree days, when we thought we were indestructible.

Tennis Courts. I could afford it some days. If not, we just played in other parts of the park.

Putting green. At the Toll Brae gate.

But it was more than just a sum of its parts.

We literally played there for days on end, and never got bored. If we did, we'd tease the 'Parkie"; our resident maligned Park Attendant, with his dark overall and name tag. And he'd chase us.

I remember cut grass. Blue skies. Fresh chips in newspaper. Carefree laughter.

I remember friends smiling faces. And the echo in that rain shelter.

And you know what? I can't remember a single bully in that park. Not one time that I had to run, or hide, or avoid the 'bad guy'.

Maybe that memory is rose-tinted. I don't care.

I'm keeping it.

Gorebridge Shops

I remember some of the shops in Gorebridge, but obviously not them all.

Let me see if we can take a walk and I can mention a few with my own recollections, and maybe jog some memories;

(From north to south; Edinburgh side (Arniston) to Country side, (Birkenside))

The Store Bakery

'Doon the brae' from the Arniston store. I think that's where the Arniston Miners is now. Big stairs into a big redbrick building.

I remember buying bread, and paper-wrapped butter.

The Store

Oh boy. The vacuum tubes to take away your money, and return with your change. You could buy anything there, from a loaf of bread to blinds for your windows. It's still there, and it still makes me shiver when I go inside.

Ben Millers Sweetshop

For some reason I never liked Ben Miller's shop. When we were going to the pictures at Dundas Hall, I always went to...

Minnie Pinkman's (see later chapter)

The view from the church (right) north to Minnies and
Edinburgh. Photo; Graham & Liz Dixon.

Then a long walk past the church, then Gorebridge
School, then past Arniston Rangers ground, past the
Scout/Cub Hut…

Ramage's Newsagents
I remember Jean Ramage from my class in Greenhall,
sitting behind me in French… her and Aileen Wood, if I
remember.

Abie (Abe) Broons
Clothier extraordinaire. They had all the school ties,
socks, blazers and badges. Shoewear, shirts… the lot.
Helped by his bonnie missus, Jennie Aird. They lived up the
top road from us, next to Christine Crane. (Don't get me
started on Christine Crane…)
Then down the hill, past the free Church, Police
Station, Saint Pauls, then the high street.

Dobsons
Up the hill a bit to the left stood Dobsons; Ice cream,
with chocolate sprinkles and raspberry sauce, and all the
Hendry's lemonade flavors. Mum knew someone in there,
maybe Nancy Cox?

Gorebridge Main Street, about 1968. Photo; Graham &
Liz Dixon

Then, going down the left side of the street....

Jim Stewarts bros's Butchers... (extreme left above)..
No, it wasn't Aytons, that was further down.

Hay's the grocers; Fruit 'n' Veg shop, (left, green).

Leslie's Newsagents, we got papers there every week,
and my comics, of course.

The-Ta-Latey (?? Spelling?) dentists... oh boy too
many stories from there. A huge black guy, who could
hardly speak English.

Veitch's Bakery
Oh man, trifles, apple charlotte's, strawberry tarts, this
was a good baker, and if I remember rightly, they had a van
come round the housing scheme too.

Lipton's Grocery Store
I remember getting a Zulu Gun here, a blowpipe for
sticky rubber darts.

Rossi's Café

Grant's Drapers

The Burns Club

Chemist David Leitch.

Aytoun's Butchers…. The best one

Post Office

Bank

I think I lost the art of concentration after the newsagents and Bakery; hard to look up when you've got the newest *Beano* or *Dandy*, and a powdery Apple Charlotte in your hands.

On the right side of the street…
Brunton's (in pic, far right) pub across the street… I don't care what name was on the door, we always called it Bruntons.

Whitey's Ironmongers
(Above; behind bus-shelter, mid right) A man with a huge crimson birthmark on his cheek (perhaps Davie Gibb?). But by God, he knew where every screw, nut and bolt were. There was a certain smell in that shop… oil, and new metal.

Nichol's newsagents

Frankie Todd's Bike Shop
(Again across the street, behind the bus shelter)

A Knitting, Wool Shop Sarah Walls/Adams

And others, but like I said, my head was churning with crumbly apple charlotte, and my head was in a comic, so didn't pay that much attention.

Gorebridge High street from the very bottom (South), looking back up the street.

As you can see, it's a fair step hill.

The photographer, Robert Ramsay is standing on Powdermill Road to take the shot.

(Remember, named after the Gunpowder factory, just further down the road.)

Newspapers

Seems a bit obvious to say, but newspapers used to be great.

Yes, I know they were fine for reading, and before the advent of television, you got all the information in the world through your newspaper.

Your newspaper told you the news.

It told your parents the people who had died that week.

Television listings, football scores, personal ads for bikes and hi-fi and stuff.

The usual newspaper stuff.

But newspapers were great for SO many other things;

Drying boots

A newspaper crumpled into wet shoes or boots, would dry them out in no time, and let them keep their shape too.

Paper Mache

There was nothing like building a model at home or at school with paper Mache. We'd spend ages tearing it into small strips, then would come the mixing of the obligatory wallpaper paste. We made mountains, buildings, volcanoes.

Lining drawers

Great at the time, because no one could afford proper drawer liners, and even better a year later when mum would re-new the liners, and we got to see all the old news; almost like a time capsule.

Chip wrappings

There is no taste like potato chips from the local chippie. Here's the perfect situation. A chilly dark night; a bit of a 'nip' in the air. Full moon, lighting the sky with big cumulus clouds scudding by. Haggis and chips, wrapped up in newspaper, and when you open the paper, you remember that you told the guy in the chip shop "Plenty Sauce; I like chips with my sauce!" The vinegar based brown sauce hits your nostrils like they'd not smelled food in years. The chips are still a bit hot, you have to blow on them, and the poke (bag) warms your other hand. Marvelous.

Carpet underlay

43

I can still remember lifting carpet in mums house, and there was newspaper sheets under it from years gone by.

Paper sticks

Now this is a stretch I admit, but I was there, I made them, and they worked. With a very primitive coal fire in the house, we'd rarely let it go all night, as it just wouldn't burn long enough. So every morning, we'd clean out the ashes, and light a new fire. When we ran out of wood kindling, we made paper sticks. Sheets of newspaper, rolled together, then criss-cross folded into each other, and put on the fire. Coal on top, and light the paper. The paper was so tightly rolled that eventually the coal caught fire. Amazing.

The Pictures (Cinema)

Gorebridge had a cinema, (now a couple of houses) between the chemist at the bottom of Barleyknowe Lane, and the Goth Tavern.

Called "Dundas Hall", the land had been donated by the Earl of Dundas himself. I was reminded by Lynn Slight that we called it the 'Fleapit'; I do recall the carpets being kinda sticky.

Dundas Hall, after it closed. The men dismantling the roof.

It was simply "The Picture House". (The Pictur' Hoose) And I still call the cinema; 'the pictures' to this day.

It was a large imposing building, and I remember being taken by my parents to see many blockbusters of the day; Shenandoah, Doctor Zhivago, The Green Berets, and many more.

David Matear, who used to stay four doors down from my Papa Hall, told me that the last film to be shown at Dundas Hall was "Krakatoa, East of Java". The poster was turned round, and "Closed" written on the back.

According to David, Derek Joyce was the projectionist, and Olive Barnowski worked in the shop.

When we got to about eight years old, we got the privilege of going ourselves, on Saturday mornings; just children. Of course we had to go in groups, and we had to promise to stay with the group, but you have to remember this was a bunch of eight year olds walking almost a mile through 'enemy territory', past Gorebridge Primary School, and crossing the 'main road' to get to the actual cinema.

The picture house actually sold sweets and drinks, but we never bought them. At the bottom of the hill (Barleyknowe Lane), was a small sweetshop, owned by a wizened old crow of a woman called Minnie Pinkman. Her son, Archie, had a barber shop at the back of the sweetshop, and I always was taken there by my dad to get our hair cut. The barbers smelled of cigarette smoke and Brylcreme. He always smoked a cigarette when he cut hair. Archie was a pal of dad's and he played the pipes in the Borthwick Pipe Band; he was important.

Chemists, Minnie Pinkmans, Ben Millers, Picture House.

Minnie was the firmest, sweetest lady on the planet, and I remember her looking about a hundred and sixty. She would give you extra, but you wouldn't dare be cheeky, she didn't put up with it. She'd tell your dad...

We'd take our money, (or a couple of Hendry's lemonade bottles, worth thruppence or something) and stand in line to be served. Apart from the usual sweets, Minnie's was full of huge glass jars with red plastic screw lids. She had boiled sweets of every variety under the sun. We would choose from the bottles, asking for just two or three, till our small paper bag on the scales hit the limit of our cash. Then she'd smile and balance the long smoking cigarette between her fingers and put an extra couple in.

We'd wait in the shop till everybody had been served, then all wave goodbye to Minnie, and go down the road to the pictures.

Cartoons, then serial shows; cowboys or Buck Rogers, then the big film. Tarzan, or something. Batman and Robin were big, and I remember Casey Jones too.

And who could forget those Lassie films?

But the biggest ones of all; the two Doctor Who films; Peter Cushing fighting the marauding Daleks.

Daleks; even the name now makes a wee boy inside me shiver.

When we left the pictures, exiting into the daylight once more, we played Daleks, or Tarzan, or John Wayne (or whatever else we had watched) all the way home. I swear it took hours to get there.

Just think of that today… a bunch of eight year olds, walking miles, away for hours, and our parents not giving one thought of it.

(I can still remember sticking two cardboard boxes together, and climbing inside; instant Dalek.)

When I think of it, at weekends and holidays, as we grew older, our 'excursions' grew more 'gallus' (Scots; self-confidently daring).

We took picnics to the park (the one mentioned earlier) and it was further away than the Pictures. We played on the swings and chute, and we took our tennis rackets and balls for a game on the courts (if we had money) or just the grass.

We ate our picnics on the manicured lawns, and no one bothered us.

The park was over a mile and a half from our homes.

We went down the 'glen'; a river glen of the twisting Gore Water, and played in the woods. We skipped stones across the water, and tried to catch minnows. We always brought something home.

In spring, we got frogspawn, and had tanks of tadpoles and frogs at home or in the greenhouse.

In summer we just played; the woods welcomed us, and we felt safe. We hung from Tarzan rope swings that other kids had left. Some of those went out over the water, they were scary. Sometimes we fell in, but we never got hurt.

In autumn we collected chestnuts, and had 'conker' fights.

(String with a large knot at the end, threaded through the chestnut. One person would hold theirs out, and the antagonist would take a swing. The winner would call his chestnut (conker) a 'one-er'. (It had smashed one opponent).

I remember having a 'forty-three-er' (It had smashed forty-three other, lesser conkers); this was one bad-ass chestnut. As big as a golf ball, soaked in vinegar, and baked for a few minutes in the oven.

(A recipe/tradition passed down for generations)

Then, in its forty-fourth fight, it met its match, and the shell cracked. I was back to square one.

We didn't need I-pads. We didn't need computers.

It was a different time, I almost wrote 'innocent time', but I stopped myself… we were no innocents.

We played pranks, not as bad as our dads had, but we still go up to stuff.

'Down the Glen' was about two miles from home.

And we'd be about ten years old.

Wow.

Me, at 13, wee brother Kevin, and dad's Alton
Greenhouse at 56 MacLean Place.
We sold the house back in 2011, the Greenhouse still
stood.

The 1968 Hurricane

It wasn't as though the storm had no warning.

January had been generally mild, temperatures above normal. The doomsayers were looking for the biggest 'doom'. There was some light snow in southern central England on Saturday 6th, but nothing significant.

Then, on the 8th, the snow fell, affecting the whole south east of England. From Redruth in Cornwall, to Swansea, South Wales, all reported heavy snow falls. Snow fell in blankets from Southampton to Manchester. By the next morning in some areas there were drifts ten feet deep, with a foot over most of Wales.

This was a slow moving Hurricane.

With no morning AM television, every school morning, almost every home tuned into the radio. Mums used it for the news, or the weather, and the kids wanted the music.

The Beatles were number one, with their hit "Hello Goodbye"; it had been there for six weeks.

Early morning, January 15th, we children in the east rose as normal. We eat our Kellogg's cornflakes or Weetabix, then toast and marmalade. There had been talk for the last few days about a storm; a hurricane, that was advancing north, along the western shores of Britain.

But we were in the east, separated by sixty long miles, many mountains, and a cultural divide bigger than Saturn.

Now, to say that we didn't give much of a hoot to what Glasgow was going through would be an understatement.

I, on the east coast, at age 9, didn't give ONE FLYING feather what was going on in Glasgow.

They weren't our immediate friends.

They weren't our immediate relatives.

And they were the football teams we loved to hate.

So… all was well in the lands of the east.

BUT… the reporters on the radio were on the ball….

They called our mothers to the speakers….

"Now we've received reports of strong winds. Children should hold hands with their friends on the way to school."

Yeah. It's true. I remember it well. We were instructed to "Hold Hands" in a Hurricane.

I'm now living in Kansas, USA, and we have basements that we flood to if there's hint of weather. Nowadays we drive our children to school if the journey is just hundreds of yards!

This, in 1968, was a three quarter mile walk, between two rows of houses, shedding huge concrete roof tiles like a thousand people throwing Frisbees.

We were asked to hold hands.

And we did.

I was nine, Lynn next door was the same, and her wee brother was seven. The Weir brothers were there and many more. Our mums stood at our garden gates that morning directing the operation, like sirens in a stormy sea.

"Hold hands now!" they urged as we passed.

(They'd heard it on the radio too.)

We did.

Although our pawkies (knitted mittens) made it difficult sometimes.

Soon, there wasn't room on the pavement for us all, so as our number grew, we walked down the middle of the street. That quiet, hurricane windy, street.

Like the Magnificent Seven walking into town.

I remember there was no rain, but the wind was swirling round us, buffeting and trying to knock us over.

And it was dark; much darker than normal. The sky, filled with blustery clouds as it was, seemed almost brown in tint.

Whilst roof tiles were being hurled amongst us, and crashing on the streets, we walked to school... holding hands, and 'blessed'.

I remember walking over the debris; tree branches and irregular triangles of thick roof tile, half an inch thick.

Smashed black slates, as the road turned the corner.

It was an interesting walk.

51

And not one ounce of fear, from anyone.

I also remember a curious feeling of belonging. I had my friends around me, and everything was going to be fine. It was almost a feeling of inner peace as I held hands. I'm not trying to impose a 'rosy-spectacles' viewpoint, but I remember a kind of domed shield over us that day. I feeling of complete invincibility.

That evening, as we watched the BBC news, Reporting Scotland made bleak viewing.

20 dead.

More than 300 injured.

2000 homeless.

Soldiers on the street to help clear the rubble.

250,000 homes damaged.

Winds of 117mph hitting Tiree.

Winds over 100mph measured all over Scotland.

The strongest winds since 1884. (The worst storm since records began)

And we walked to school, holding hands, grinning,...... oblivious.

People evacuated the tall Glasgow flats when they began to sway in the wind.

Power failed in Glasgow, leaving the WHOLE CITY in darkness.

Edinburgh sent 150 troops to Glasgow to help in the rescue work.

Off the east coast of Scotland, an oil drilling rig called Sea Quest was set adrift in stormy seas.

The storm moved on to Denmark, where 9 people died.

30 more died repairing the damage from the storm, 11 falling off roofs.

Frankie Vaughn did a special concert to raise money for the homeless, at least seven ships sank as a result of the storm.

From that day forth, as we walked through the woods and forests, we catalogued the years as pre-68 or after.

Huge trees all over the country, knocked over like grass; their huge circular root systems rising for all to see.

An estimated half million trees fell that day, in Scotland alone.

And we walked to school, holding hands.

Of Roman Camps and Scottish Castles

About a mile and a half from our street lay a Roman marching camp.

At least that's what it said on the Ordinance Survey map.

I remember going there as a very young kid, maybe six or seven, with dad looking for goldfinches or yellowhammers. Later we kids went there, not alone of course, and we'd see strange stones with strange markings, and collect them... from the Roman Camp.

Roman Artifacts sitting in my bedroom. Magical.

Of course, a year later we'd venture farther, and find we hadn't reached the camp yet, and the stones were bogus, but we didn't care.

Then we found the camp.

Arches of stone in regular buildings, tunnels to explore, a tower to climb; it seemed an enchanted place oozing in history.

Until a while later when someone explained it was an old lime kiln from the late 1800's...

The same lime kiln, 2012. Photo Robert Ramsay

Then, one day we found the camp.

Not another false-start; the real camp.

Huge concentric square ridges in the ground two thousand years old.

To be honest, it wasn't much to look at, but it was sighted on the side of the hill near Mayfield, and it provided a great view of Edinburgh.

We had more fun at the lime kiln pretending. Ah well.

Then one year, Mum and Dad bought me a bike.

A real road bike, not a three wheeler.

It was red, with white mudguards, and two brakes, one for each wheel; I can honestly say that I was impressed.

Dad taught me how to ride, keeping balanced and stuff.

I can still remember him letting the back of the seat go, and how crazily I wobbled at first, bouncing on the grass up the back field.

I learned to do a lot of things up the 'back field'.

Archery, golf, bonfires, football.

We even re-invented the Atlatl (spear thrower).

We got our dads heavier garden canes, five feet long, made the flights out of playing cards, and used a short piece of string to launch them. They went farther than we could ever throw them; we thought we'd invented a new science.

We didn't know the Aztecs or Incas had invented them.

We called them 'flight-eys'.

Atlatl; Blah.

Anyway… bikes…

Our bikes meant we could venture farther from home… and we did.

Trips for wood for the bonfire, dragging the trees home by bike.

Trips looking for stuff for the countless school projects we had to do.

And trips to Crichton Castle (Three miles away, at around seven-nine years old… not that we ever told our folks where we were going. We just told them where we'd been, *after* we'd got home.)

Crichton Castle, Midlothian. Photo Robert Ramsay

Man, that castle still looks great.

I remember one time we went (with a picnic of course). We sat on the slope (above) and told ghost stories of the men who would rise from the marsh at the bottom of the hill.

I remember getting quite carried away with those tales.

Birds and Eggs

At one time, dad kept canaries in his shed, and a selection of wild birds too. Will Slight (Mister Slight to me, father of Lynn and James) did the same in his aviary next door.

He'd breed them and always meant to 'show' them in competitions, but I don't remember him actually getting to that stage.

I helped clean out the cages (yup, I fell for it, and did the dirty work).

I re-filled the water feeders, and topped up the seed trays. The pastime was very common back then, and I looked Will Slight's birds one summer when they were on holiday. I got an *Airfix* model boat as my reward when they came home; RMS Mauretania, I still remember.

I used to go walks with dad, to catch Greenfinches, or the beautiful Goldfinch or Yellowhammer. We'd put 'sticky-sticks' in the fruit bushes, and go back the next day to see what we'd caught.

I also remember using a glass pipette to feed chicks.

Keeping and breeding birds also gave rise to an 'egg collection', and dad already had a few. Wrapped in cotton wool, we'd bring them out some nights and dad would 'test' me on the different varieties. We bought the "*Observers book of Birds Eggs*", and compared them.

Dad's cousin Jack Carson had a huge collection, including many hawks (illegal) and huge Swan's eggs (VERY Illegal).

We tried homing pigeons, but they were more difficult to keep, and the bother of getting them down from the roof, and into the hut at night became too much.

Pretty soon all we used birds for was feathers for tying fishing flies.

The Burnside Road Store and Hammy's

Burnside Road shops lay at the bottom of the hill to Stobhill School. We passed it every day.

And if we had money, we went into Hammy's (Actually Hamilton's sweet shop/grocers) and we spent our pennies on Bazooka Joes or anything else that took our fancy. An empty Barr's bottle was worth a few pence, and if you found one on the road, you immediately felt rich.

If we had no money, we'd chum (accompany) our friends in, on the off chance that Hammy himself was feeling generous.

One day, however, this warm, chummy arrangement stopped. Next door was the Burnside Road Co-op; a proper grocery store.

Somehow we found out that we could buy cooking chocolate cheaper than regular bars of the stuff.

And this stuff wasn't in squares either.

Missus Rogers (Derek Rogers Mum) would chip a block off for us, and weigh it.

It was so big and clumsy, we couldn't eat it. We could only peel back the greaseproof paper wrapping and gnaw.

Like mice in a pantry.

Gnaw it till we could close the deal.

I still remember that slightly oily feeling, and that rich sugary taste.

My 2 First Days at School (7 years apart)

I still remember my first day at Stobhill Primary School, Gorebridge.

I was five years old, and felt so far out of my comfort zone, I just wanted to run home (not that I knew what a comfort zone was, of course, but I felt out of it anyway.).

It was September nineteen sixty-four.

Stobhill Primary School, Primary 4? Circa 1968-ish?
Bruce McGuff, Jim Murray, Neil McGuff, Ian Hall (me), ??, Sandy Faulds, Tommy Young, Andrew Birrell, Charles Falconer, ??, Carol Young, Christine Gill, Lynn Slight, Anne Haining, Sandra Black, Colin Renton, Valerie Sinclair, Ruth Weir, Christine Nohar, Valerie Reid, Leslie Wilson, Gail Robson, Carol Sheppard, ??, Ann Dryesdale.

There had been no 'getting used to it' like we have today. No nursery class, no orientation, no mums coming with us and sitting beside us, nothing.

It was BAM! You're in school, kiddo!

Mum took me first day, initially taking my hand, but after others joined the 'parade' along the road, I walked with the other kids. Some of them were also having their first day; Lynn from next door, Christine from over the road, so it wasn't like I was totally alone, of course. The five year olds were all in the same boat, and our mums chatted amongst themselves as we walked.

The mums took us to the infant's door, and put our coats on our pegs in the cloakroom.

I recall going back there when I was older, and those racks were so low to the ground, it was so funny.

I remember on that first day, standing at the classroom door, staring in awe.

The desks were in clumps of four or six, facing each other in groups. Some of us even faced away from the blackboard. There was color everywhere; the walls were covered in children's paintings and printed pictures, the floor had big boxes round the edges of books, crayons, blocks and plasticine. Stuck on the huge windows were colored designs and shapes, and the window ledges were filled with potted plants, all flowering.

We were filled with the expectation of play.

Our teacher was a great woman; Miss Watson.

Miss Watson, not missus. She seemed middle aged to me even then, and she continued teaching in that school till she retired. Every kid in the village from five to fifty knew her, and said 'hello' as they passed. She was a grand lady. I remember her really fondly. She stayed in Gorebridge until she died. Hundreds turned out at the funeral.

So, through those big windows, we watched our mums walk away across the playground, and Miss Watson called our attention. She told us her name, and made us say it back to her. I remember every morning in life began the same way. We'd enter the classroom with her holding the door open, and take our seats, hooking our schoolbags (satchels) on the back of our chairs. When we were all inside, she'd close the door and stand in front of the class.

"Good Morning children." She'd say.

And we'd sing "Good Morning Miss Watson!" with huge smiles on our faces.

After a little bit of teaching, it would be 'milk time'. A crate of small milk bottles sat in the corner of the class waiting for us. Each was stamped "1/3 pint". In the winter it was fine, the milk would be cold, but in summer, it wasn't. I had to force myself to drink the tepid stuff, and I think that's where my dislike of warm milk began.

If someone was absent, there would be extra. There was always someone wanting more. If you'd been especially good, you'd get an extra bottle.

Incidentally, free milk in primary schools lasted till 1971, when Margaret Thatcher, then the Education Secretary, cancelled free school milk for those children over 7 years old. It earned her the nickname "Maggie Thatcher, school milk snatcher".

Anyway, after play-time (15 min outside break), Miss Watson announced that the headmaster, Mr. Jamieson, would be along to visit us.

When he came to the door and knocked, we sat very nervously. We needn't have bothered, of course, he was a great man, and by the end of our seven years at the school, we loved him dearly (despite his nickname "the crust" that we learned years later).

He came into our classroom, and we sat with great reverence. He wore his flowing black graduation gown. It was a special occasion.

He welcomed us to the school, and took the class register. One by one, he called us up, in alphabetical order. As each kid stood in front of him, he pinned a badge on out jerseys; blue, then red, then green, then back to blue.

Every kid had a badge.

He then told us that we'd just been put in 'houses'.

It meant little to us then, but ask anyone now, in their fifties and older; they'll still remember what 'house' they were in; and the color. They probably remember what some of their friends were, because those little colored badges changed our lives.

It was a bit like the Harry Potter stories that have become so popular.

Mr. Jamieson told us the 'house' names, and told us never to forget them.

Lauder (blue); (a town in the borders, about fifteen miles from Gorebridge, not that big, but for some reason much bigger than the other two.)

Middleton (red); (a small village about 3 miles away.)

Temple; (green); (another small village, 3 miles away.)

I remember looking down at the blue badge, "Lauder", I pondered. I wasn't exactly sure what on earth it was, but I knew that I had been given access to a very special club. I looked around the class. I was five. I didn't even know half of the kids yet, but those with blue badges were suddenly my friends.

There was a kinship, and a feeling of belonging.

The headmaster told us we could buy extra badges for our other clothes. Within weeks, I remember having one on my blazer, and on my heavy woolen dufflecoat.

Just like in Harry Potter, yet forty years before it was written, we had 'houses' that we belonged to. And sometimes it meant the world.

For the next seven years, every time we did anything remotely 'team like', our teachers would shout "House!" and we ran to three corners of the room. Pretty soon, we didn't even need the badges. We all knew our house members.

Nearly fifty years later, I still remember some of my friends, and the color of the badges they wore. Memory sure is a strange thing.

Along the years, some kids had the nerve to switch Houses, and you know who you are!

I stayed in Lauder through sports days, football games, class projects, and class outings.

We were a fine bunch of people.

Seven years later, when I went to High school, for our first day, our Primary School houses were gone forever.

The small Stobhill Primary School was so easily forgotten.

~ ~ ~

Greenhall High looked massive to us on our first day.

Greenhall High School took in three big Primary Schools, and maybe three or four small ones (funnily enough, including Middleton and Temple)

So, seven years later, I went through the 'first day at school' all over again.

No mum walked us to the gates, and I walked a mile to get there, all downhill, mostly with the same kids I'd shared a class with for the last seven years.

When we reached the gates, every single kid was older than us, and they all looked bigger, meaner.

There were signs directing the "First Year" students to the Assembly room.

I remember thinking that I had turned from Schoolchild into Student instantly.

But it seemed more... there was an undercurrent of change; we'd suddenly changed from the oldest kids at primary school, the 'big ones' the school prefects... to the youngest, smallest.

It was different, all right; Instead of twenty, five-year-olds sitting in a classroom, there were over a hundred and fifty of us, standing in the Greenhall Assembly Room. We stood, the clump of Stobhill Primary kids, looking around us at the many strange faces. I knew some of the Gorebridge Primary boys from Cub Scouts, and I nodded and smiled. Sandy Allan, Jim Robertson.

This time, the headmaster walked up the steps to the stage.

"My name is Mister Angus.", he announced.

William Angus was a lovely man if you didn't cross him. He lived in Carrington, and always reminded me of the actor Iain Cuthbertson.

His speech was considerably longer than the previous one. I remember he talked about doing homework, and us all going to be developing dandruff with being indoors 'swotting' for exams so much. He waved his belt at us, and warned us what would happen if we misbehaved.

I'd had the belt a couple of times from 'the crust', but Angus's thick leather thing had a split running along half its length. It did look menacing.

"So, I'll announce the classes." He said, holding a huge sheet of paper in front of him. "Class One A. You will stand in line by Mrs. Young here on my right. She will be your register Teacher."

I had no idea what a 'Register Teacher' was, but I remember Mrs. Young. I was instantly impressed. She was slim, with long, straight, brown/red hair.

And really good looking too; maybe thirty/thirty-five?

Well, Mr. Angus began to read the names, boys first, in alphabetical order. Apart from the few from cub scouts, they were all strangers.

"Ian Hall."

Crap, I thought, "That's me.", and walked forward to the three or four boys already in line in front of Mrs. Young. Reassuringly, they all had a kind of 'out-of-my-depth' look on their faces.

"David Hogg", was announced next. Easy for me to remember, I still am in touch.

Mr. Angus got to the end of the boys for 1A.

No other boys from Stobhill were called. I was on my own.

Girls next, and the only one from Stobhill was Lesley Wilson. I remember her, she was so cute.

Slowly the rest of the twelve-year-olds were divided into classes from 1A to 1F. Halfway through the ceremony, I realized that we were being split on 'cleverness'.

So, I was in the top class. No one said it out loud, but soon enough we all knew it.

Once it was all done, Angus said his last, and Mrs. Young led us out of the assembly room. We followed her cute backside in file along corridors, and Mrs. Young pointed out the school office, Headmasters room, cloakrooms and toilets.

We all took seats in her classroom.

All the desks were lined pointing to the front, in pairs. The boy next to me looked as sheepish as I felt. "Ian Hall; Stobhill." I said. "Tommy Symonds; Middleton." Came the reply. I sat with my new friend, and looked around the room.

Bare walls.

It was like a prison cell.

It turned out that we'd decorate it with our English work over the year, but Mrs. Young had taken all last year's stuff down.

On that first day, it felt strange. Very stark.

Mrs. Young said that every morning we'd meet here, in her class to take Registration. Then we'd go to our classes for lessons.

She turned the blackboard round to our schedule.

Wow, that was an eye opener.

Each day was divided into eight 45 min periods.

I looked at the subjects; Chemistry, Art, French... FRENCH? Maths (there was a lot of maths) and Arithmetic, Physics (I had NO idea what physics was) English.

Our English teacher was Mrs. Young herself, the head of the English department. It seemed that day, that 1A were getting taught by a lot of 'heads of departments'.

Geography, History, Physical Education, Religious Studies.

It was a lot to take in.

There was one for girls, which had cooking and 'Home Economics', and one for the boys with Woodwork and Metalwork.

But we duly copied it all down onto a blank Photostat she gave us.

It was all very serious, terrifying, very official; very compartmentalized.

I also remember, us getting a little too chatty. Mrs. Young roared; "Quieten Down!" with a clipped, authoritative bark.

There was an edge to her voice that I'd never heard before.

An edge that bore ill will.

I shut up immediately, knowing that the world had changed. Our teachers in Stobhill primary had never had that sharpness to their tone.

Then she said she would read out the 'houses'.

Buccleugh was blue.

Dalhousie was green.

Melville was red.

Lothian was yellow.

I was a staunch blue twelve-year-old Lauder man, and cringed in anticipation at my new soon-to-be-allotted house.

"Ian Hall; Buccleugh". Mrs. Young said.

I smiled.

I sat at my desk, amongst total strangers, outwardly trembling, but inside, I was warm and cozy with the knowledge that my old blue badges could still be worn.

I had one in my schoolbag, and I determine to wear it as soon as I could get a chance.

The Great Stovie Debate

(Started as a post in the Greenhall High School Facebook page)

Stovies is a traditional Scottish dish, basically made from the left-overs of another meal.

There is a possibility that the word Stovies comes from the French "étouffée", to steam, and it would make for a good piece of table trivia, but no one can be certain. Personally I doubt it.

Jim Slight made the point that it was a dish cooked on the 'stove'; 'stove tatties' became stovies.

It is, however, commonly accepted that it's a Monday dish, re-hashing the left-overs of an extravagant Sunday roast, and that would lead to the meat content in most of the recipes.

So for the traditional Monday cooking, it is based in the old beef gravy, and all the components are either cooked in this gravy or heated up in it. Because of this, every component of the dish soaks in the gravy, heightening the taste.

To recreate the dish from scratch, in its very basic form, we have beef gravy, onions, and potatoes. That's the basis of the dish, and many would argue that's it… don't add anything else. That's the way some households had the dish. However, that's not holding up the traditional conception of using up left-overs.

In the old days of the dish's history, any addition would be based on whatever left-overs you had, added to the mixture and heated up.

In our house, to add meat/proteins, my mum would brown some minced beef, and sliced or chopped sausage. I've also heard of chicken, turkey and more commonly corned beef (Popular at the time, tinned/canned).

Adding vegetables also enhances taste, and keeps the traditionalists happy; my mum added chopped carrots and turnip/rutabaga.

I put these additions on the Greenhall High School Facebook site recently, and got all kinds of friendly, yet vehement comments. Seems everyone had their own version, and that became a family tradition. And anything different from the home favorite is sacrilege.

But whatever the mixture above, the bulk of the dish is potatoes; perhaps two to five times the quantity of the rest of the pot; anything to eke out the left-overs and feed the family. Cooked real slow as to not burn the contents at the bottom of the pan, it simmered for a good hour, gently bringing the dish to fruition.

I even remember mum sometimes putting a potato masher through it, just to make it more mushy.

In my house I always garnished the steaming plate with some kind of ketchup, or broon or fruity HP sauce.

Wonderful.

It makes a mockery of the dish's primary intent to see it included in some Scottish fine dining restaurants, but I've seen cod or mackerel used as the protein, served with a fresh salad, hot oatcakes and beetroot.

But it gets worse, there's even a casserole version, topped with roasted cheese. "Serve with a sprinkling of chopped chives or parsley"… OH PLEASE.

Stick to the basics, and it'll be braw.

Granny and Papa Hall

Dad's mum was as thin as you could get without blowing away, but Granny Hall was tall. I don't remember how tall she was, but she always said I got my height from the Harrison side of the family; her side, and I got to six foot three. My brother, Kevin, is six one. Both of us dwarfed dad, and stood a foot taller than mum, so maybe Granny Hall had been right.

At her funeral, I found out that the Harrisons are all tall, even the women.

But back then, there wasn't an ounce of meat on her bones, probably because she smoked those Benson & Hedges sticks, but by God she could cook an apple pie. I've never tasted better, and I'm a bit of a connoisseur.

(All those Veitch's Apple Charlotte's)

She used to have to cook three pies at one time, tiered up in the oven; one for the neighbors to share, one for us, and one for themselves. All on circular, well beaten, clear Pyrex plates.

She even gave the crust recipe to my mum, and mum could cook! But she never quite got it right.

I always thought that she missed something out of the recipe, just to flummox her. Granny did have a wee bit of 'devil' inside her.

She must have been a bit of a looker back in her day, because Papa passed by on a new life in New York, just to be with her. He was serious too. Had a job with a cousin's shipbuilders, had the ticket paid for, and had his entry visa. We've still got the proof. He was twenty six or something.

One thing I remember her telling us about was playing tennis. Papa used to watch her play, and that was back in the thirties, when the women had to wear long skirts to play. She must have stolen his heart quickly.

Tennis.

Well, every June, Wimbledon Fortnight hit BBC television. It was aired morning, day and evening, even back in the late sixties when I was a youngster.

Black and white.

Granny and papa Hall lived at 91 Newhunterfield, the main road from Arniston to the A9 Galashiels road (Post Road). David Matear, who grew up just four doors down from the Halls, reminded me that Newhunterfield was called the 'Toll Brae'. Perhaps because the pub at the bottom was the "Auld Toll", I don't really know.

Anyway, if we visited Granny's house for apple pie when the tennis was on, we had to dish it ourselves.

Granny would put the brown leather pouffe about six feet from the TV. She'd be down on her knees behind it, leaning, watching and smoking. Papa's tea was made during the news, and if it didn't quite make it, she'd simply switch the whole cooker off (Papa was hopeless at cooking) and catch up with it later.

Carry-outs were a thing saved for rainy days, but Granny's house got its fair share of fish 'n' chips during Wimbledon.

If we talked too loud behind her, she'd snap; "Shut-up!" repeating the word as long as it took for us to get the message. I thought it was funny. I loved tennis too. Mum thought it was rude, but never let told anyone so. Granny would have bit her head off.

She watched it religiously, and cheered every nationality. There wasn't a bone of racism in her regarding tennis.

In these heady days of Andy Murray (Scottish) and his record-breaking Wimbledon win in 2013, I imagine her in heaven, watching his progress with a stubborn nationalistic pride. If an angel told her to calm down, I can imagine the "Shut-up!" he would receive.

Papa Hall worked in the Coal Mining Industry, just like Dad. As far as I remember him, he was always retired. He pottered around in the garden, but his garage and shed were full of woodworking tools.

If he had any spare time, he'd sit, pipe in mouth, straightening nails with a hammer, on a small vice.

He made swords for my cousin and I to fight with. He even made me a wooden Bismark Battleship. It was incredibly detailed.

But best of all were the air-guns.

Granny and Papa had two sons; Andrew (father of me and Kevin) and George (Father of Alan, David and Robin).

He had two air-guns which we could ogle at, and he had promised them to me and Alan (as the eldest of each family).

When we got old enough (ten I think) we actually got to keep them. I got first pick, and we fired pellets out of these till you'd thought the barrel was wasted.

I have no idea what happened to those guns, but boy did we have some fun out of them.

Granny and Papa Dyer

Granny Dyer, mum's mum, died when I was eleven, but my memories of her and our trips to Edinburgh to visit her, are as fresh in my mind as any.

Granny and Papa Dyer lived in Bruntsfield, Edinburgh. Quite a posh area, really, and their first floor flat looked out onto the sixteenth hole at Bruntsfield golf course. It was just a 'pitch and putt' course, but it still looked great.

Granny Dyer's house is first floor corner, on the left.

Dad would work all week, and on Saturday, he'd be away on the bus, fishing the Gala Water or the Tweed near Galashiels. So, left on our own, Mum and I would go to see Granny Dyer. We went almost every Saturday.

The routine was terrific.

First we'd get dressed up; nice clothes, not the play stuff of the week, we're talking blazer and trousers here. We'd get a bus, and despite the smoking upstairs, I'd try to persuade mum to let me sit on the top deck. It seemed much more exciting

We'd get off at the Edinburgh bus station (which was cool, SO FULL of buses, and a café, and a newspaper stand), and Papa Dyer was a bus driver, so sometimes we'd see him.

Then we'd walk down to Princes Street. Edinburgh Castle was there. Princess Street gardens, the Train Station. There was just so much for a young boy to see.

We would always go to Woolworths on the corner, and I would always get some Dolly Mixture, measured out for weight in a small white bag.

A paper poke.

Sometimes, very rarely, we'd eat lunch upstairs at the Woolies Café. Lorne Sausage in Gravy, with Mashed Tatties. It's still my favorite today, ask my wife. I have never refined it or made it 'foo-foo'.

Just flat sausage and brown beef gravy.

Then out onto Princes Street, and if my memory serves me right, an 11, 15, 16 or 23 bus up to Bruntsfield.

We'd get off the bus at the top of the 'Meadows', Edinburgh's answer to Central Park. Mum used that strange 'castle' key to open the latch to let us into the stairs, then up the worn square steps to the first floor.

I was a kid, and the steps were already worn. This place was old.

The door was huge, and had a rail and a curtain behind it.

I would hug Granny, then sit very well-mannered for what seemed like centuries until Granny let me go through the room for my new *Beezer* comic.

It was always there, and always in the same drawer every week. She never missed one.

I think I asked for it to be changed to something later, but don't recall what it was.

I read the *Beezer* for ages.

The off to the window to see the weather.

If it was dry, I'd ask permission to take two clubs and two balls downstairs to the golf course.

People never paid for their rounds of golf. It was free, and I seem to remember two 18 hole courses. No one minded a child playing around on the quiet parts.

As I got older, I played more holes, getting farther and farther from the flat.

It was stupendous.

I still remember the ribbed grips on the wooden shafts. Those clubs were old by the time I got to them; just holding them felt great.

If the weather was wet, I played Granny's 78 records, and whiled away the day listening to Guy Mitchell, and the Mikado, and all the hip tunes from the 40's and 50's.

Only bad thing was Granny's soup.

Papa Dyer liked his soup thin and runny, and boy did Granny oblige. There was always leeks in it, with lots of barley.

Sometimes Papa was there, and he took me out to do errands. When we did go out, usually I'd get something. A toy, or a model at the shop on the corner. Or a record at the store down the road.

It would be my choice.

My first was a pipe band extended play 45; "Festival Marches".

I flummoxed him the next time; I'd heard a song on the TV the night before; Italian singing sensation Rita Pavone; "The Man who makes the Music".

Pavone had recorded with Diana Ross, Paul Anka and many more.

(My research puts this at 67 or 68; I was eight,)

Craziest thing; they had it in stock.

I still remember most of the obscure song.

Once he took me to a huge indoor funfair near the station. Boy that was great.

Then Granny died, and we didn't visit Papa as much because he worked most Saturdays.

Great times.

Papa Dyer was a fine figure of a man. He fought in the desert in the war, and ended in Palestine, turning a blind eye to Jews arriving on the beaches. He told me that himself.

His regiment was one of Scotland's finest; The 'Royal Scots Greys'; famous for their charge at the Battle of Waterloo, a cavalry regiment. Of course, 'cavalry' in the desert, meant you got driven places, then fought. He had a brass horse, that he had stolen from the door of one of the stables.

It was a great memento.

Once, when mum was ill, and in hospital, I must have been in the way or maybe Papa was bored, because he took me outside.

I was fifteen, and had just got my first pair of jeans that spring; two pair of flared hand-me-downs from one of Dad's friends. I loved them

Papa got me outside the hospital and asked me what I wanted in all of life. I couldn't answer. "Come on." He enthused. "If you had lots of money right now, what would you buy?"

Only one thing came into my mind.

"A Levi Jacket."

Of course, I then had to tell him exactly what one was.

"And where would we get one?"

"Denimport." I replied, beginning to get excited. "Royal Mile."

He nodded, and led the way to a bus stop.

Now, remember I told you that he was a bus driver. Well, by now he had retired, and we stood at the bus stop, waiting for the bus.

The bus came, stopped right in front of us, and just as Papa was getting ready to step on, a cheeky chappie slipped past us and got on before us. I thought him rude, but Papa was quicker.

He grabbed the guy by the back of his collar, and pulled/jerked him physically back off the bus.

It happened in a split second, and the guy was so shocked.

"We were first sonny!" Papa said quietly but firmly, and we both got on the bus. "Hi Dave." Papa said to the driver. "Hi Jas." The driver replied, and motioned us back into the bus without paying.

I learned a lot about Papa Dyer that day. His nickname was Jas.

We got to Denimport, and I was instantly out of my league.

Denim everywhere, and very cute girls standing around waiting to serve. I was as nervous as a kitten.

Damn it if Papa didn't go right up to one and said; "This is my Grandson. He wants a Levi jacket."

We got served as quick as a flash.

Papa Dyer didn't mess around.

I loved that jacket.

Comics

I've mentioned a few so far, but it seems time to talk for a little while about comics.

Newspapers for Kids, that we bought every week.

I think it all started with the *Sunday Post*, that august very Scottish newspaper printed by D.C. Thomson in Dundee. Our parents (and every other household in Scotland) bought one every week; Wikipedia puts their circulation at nearly THREE MILLION, in a country of five million people.

"In the 1950s, when the newspaper was confined largely to Scotland, sales of the Sunday Post were so high that it was recorded in the Guinness Book of records as the newspaper with the highest per capita readership penetration of anywhere in the world."

Anyway, just off the centre pages was a 'children's section' with jokes and kid's stuff, but they had strip cartoons, very Scottish; *The Broons* and *Oor Wullie, Black Bob*, all aimed at kids, but our parents read them too.

Great stuff to look forward to on a Sunday.

I can't remember the first actual comic I read, but it was probably a Dandy or Beano.

They'd been going since the thirties, but when I got to them, they both raised my reading speed, and gave me great laughs. *The Bash Street Kids, Dennis the Menace, Minnie the Minx, Desperate Dan, Roger the Dodger, Billy Whizz, Biffo the Bear, Lord Snooty.*

Great stuff.

Others too vied for my hard-earned pennies; The Sparky, The Buster, Cor!,

Then there were the broadsheets; the pre-mentioned *Beezer*, and *Topper*.

As I grew older, leaving the kiddy comic strip behind, boys turned to the *Victor*, or the *Hotspur, Eagle* or *Hornet*, war stories, more serious topics, football; *Roy of the Rovers, Tough of the Track*, etc.

Girls graduated to the *Bunty, Tammy* and *Diana*, with more girlie stuff inside. Boys didn't even go there.

Eventually I got *TV Century 21*, which had a more sci-fi based genre, *Doctor Who*, *Fireball XL5*, *Stingray* etc.

Every year at Christmas these magazines brought out a hard cover "Annual".

I usually got one of these, or maybe more. We swapped them at school and read them all

I even bought a couple on Ebay, just to re-live the old times.

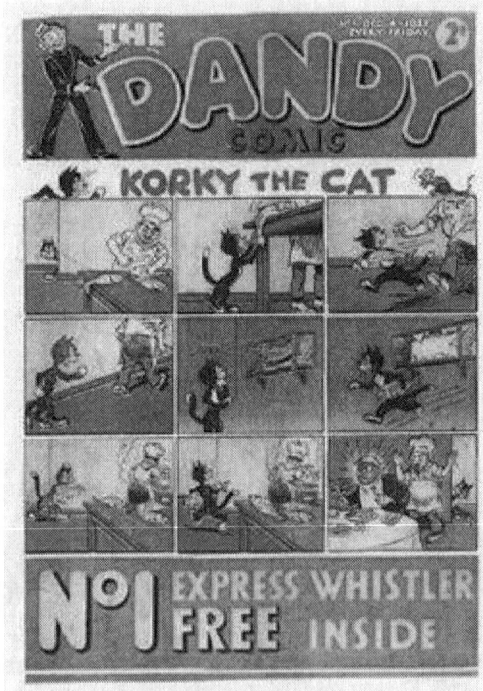

Dandy, number 1. Worth hundreds of pounds.

School Projects and Collecting Things

School Projects were weird things. Some were interesting; like airplanes. Some boring, like Dollar Castle.

For such projects, we'd split into four or five groups, and we'd 'research' stuff. I'd always pick Andrew Burrell for our projects team. First pick every time. Now even at a young age we all subconsciously knew our level of academia, and usually I was a 'project captain'. That gave me the choice of people in my team, and Andrew wasn't the best student... but he could draw. Oh boy could he draw... and that meant our project got the best pictures.

Anyway, these projects usually meant a trip sometime.

A project on Waterloo, meant a trip to the Odeon in Edinburgh for the film (movie).

Ditto on Cromwell to see the Richard Harris film.

Dollar Castle... guess where we went? Miss Johnston even took her out-of-tune guitar.

Blah.

Of course, almost every year we'd do a project on Guy Fawkes.

And collections? We'd always be collecting something or other.

First there was the personal collections.

Comics... duh.

Football cards were always on the go. Tommy Young had an uncle in London that got him Arsenal Match day programs. Boy, Tommy took some football cards for those, but I cherished them.

Then there were the 'official' school collections.

Some of those were for *Blue Peter* stuff. We collected bottle tops, clothes pegs, rubber bands, and other things to help Hospitals or dogs for the blind or something.

The esteemed Blue Peter Badge.

I'm certain the school got a *Blue Peter* badge at one point.

We even collected rosehips.

Thousands upon thousands of them, for the Rosehip Syrup Company.

We got a certificate in return.

Bonfire Time (Guy Fawkes)

When I was ten or so, back in the late sixties, going back to school in September for your 'new year' was a big thing; it usually meant a new classroom, and new teacher. As you lined up on that first day, you could actually 'feel' yourself being a year older. That newness lasted for a few weeks… you got used to the new teacher, you got your first 'group project' under your belt, then you started to act weird.

It wasn't a scary, creepy kind of weird, but there were several changes that early October brought.

First, of course, it got colder and wetter, the nights got longer, and playtime between the end of school and 'dark' got shorter.

(I'm not really sure what 'dark' meant to our parents. It was a weird thing. In summer, it was perfectly respectable to play outside till eight o'clock, or so, because it was 'light' enough. But in winter, I remember my mum calling me 'in', at five, because it was 'dark'. Parents didn't understand; 'dark' just made hide-and-seek much more interesting.)

Anyway….. Back to kids turning weird.

The first sign was that you gave every tree a second look, mentally working out if you could chop it down with your dad's sheath knife or if it would take the family axe.

Your mum started to notice that you began to collect old newspapers, and old cardboard boxes (usually filled to bursting with the old newspapers).

In our village, our normal childhood bike trips changed too. We began to categorize the trees as "arm thick", or "two arm thick".

Parts of our gardens were used as dumps for pieces of wood of every description. As the weeks advanced, the piles of paper and wood got bigger. Mums knew what was going on, Dads tried to ignore it (but locked their best wood in their sheds away from sticky fingers).

Around the third week of October, the scouring of the neighborhood moved to a bigger scale. On weekends, packs of kids armed with all kinds of chopping implements headed to their pre-determined tree targets. (Now remember here, I'm talking seven, eight, nine, ten year olds walking around town, with axes, and big foot0long knives) It took all day, and sometimes we even took packed lunches. Once the trees (usually little more than saplings, but some still twenty feet high) were chopped, they were dragged back through the streets to unsuspecting gardens, to be stored till November. I still remember dragging a thirty foot tree over two miles uphill to my home, to see it denied entrance by my dad, still shaking his head.

We found it another temporary resting place.

Little by little, our gardens took on the look of rubbish dumps. We even scoured the debris out on the curb on 'rubbish day' for anything flammable.

On Halloween, the collecting was forgotten for a day, as we raided our parent's wardrobes for anything to dress up in. Ghosts and witches roamed the streets in groups, knocking on both friend and stranger. We'd do our 'party piece' for a few sweets. We'd sing, recite Burn's poems. It only cost the folks a handful of sugar, but they got an evening of variety.

Halloween also was the day that the 'Annuals' arrived in the shops. An 'Annual' was the hard-backed version of the weekly comics. Special editions for Christmas. I got asked the same question every year.

"Do you want fireworks? Or an Annual?"

Well, I wasn't stupid. Fireworks were going to be let off anyway. Unerringly I chose the Annual, and every year I got my Victor Annual presented to me by mum. She saved tuppence a week or something to get it.

I've already mentioned that I got a couple of Victor Annuals from Ebay last month. What a hoot that was.

Anyway. The story.

The next day, November first, we got back to work. We needed to begin to move the gear to the pre-determined site, and everyone was called out to help. There had been a bonfire at the same place for five years that I knew of, built by the oldest kids.

At the 'back field' down in the corner by Jim Murray's house, we piled our cardboard boxes, till it was over our heads. We planned 'watches' on our bonfires until we were called inside by our parents. We feared the worst crowd (at the next field down) would raid our carefully collected papers for their own bonfire.

I still remember one year, we watched the Logans and the Bartons; the gang from the 'top road' dragging a huge tree. It took four or five of them to move it, and we stood, envious that they had found the mother lode. Cars had to wait till they pulled it across the street. We didn't help them.

We walked the streets, knocking on doors, asking for wood, paper, cardboard; basically anything that would burn. I remember being so frustrated that we didn't have enough.

But of course we always did.

On the evening of November fourth, the wood was moved from the hideouts. Dozens of kids carried tons of wood to their growing stacks; pieces of construction wood, scraps of balsa, rotten fence posts, and even bundles of rose and hedge clippings. One year, we even had the four walls of an old shed; dads moved them for us. Piece by piece, we piled it onto the bonfire.

On November fifth, we soaked in the story of Guy Fawkes at school, drawing pictures of Parliament burning, or tunnels full of barrels of gunpowder, or the gallows that he hung on.

It was all very well and good, but no-one really cared much.

Our thoughts were of our stacks, standing unguarded in our fields. We worried that other gang members had feigned a cold in the morning and weren't at school, set free in the afternoon to raid our still uncompleted bonfires.

We ran home from school that afternoon, not to our homes, but to our bonfires.

We needn't have worried.

Our bonfire stood like an irregular pyramid, some papers blowing in the breeze, leaving a trail across the field; It was the only day in our year that we picked up litter willingly, stuffing it back in sometimes damp cardboard boxes.

Before we even thought of fireworks, there was one task still to do.

The trees had to be moved.

One by one, we dragged them from our gardens or their hiding places to the bonfire, and set them up the side like the sides of a wigwam, criss-crossing at the top.

The girls would tell us where to position them, the boys would stand them carefully, then push them gently into place.

Exhausted, but full of nervous energy, we positioned the last of the trees, then waited on the grown-ups who had both the fireworks and the petrol to light the bonfire.

Looking up at the twenty-foot high masterpiece, we sat as one huge family; the Slights, the three Weir brothers, the Flemings, the Browlee girls, the Cornwalls, and the single kids like me, Stuart Robertson, Conrad Csysa, Jim Murray. We had all done something to get the bonfire to its completion. Older kids from the 'top road' would turn up; Alan MacGowan, Christine Crane, remembering their younger days.

It soon started to get dark. Some kids arrived with sparklers. We shared them out, and lit them from each other's. We laughed as we waved the crackling wands, signing our names into our retinas.

It was the best of times.

We watched in anticipation as the designated grown-up lit the fire. Some years the stuff was damp, sometimes sodden, but whatever the condition, the flames were soon tearing through everything we'd collected. We saw cardboard boxes, burst into flames, and pieces of wood from garden frames and fences. And as the flames licked higher, we looked up at the Guy.

Sometimes it was just a teddy bear, sometimes a full stuffed kind of person with real trousers and jacket; the offering to the memory of Guy Fawkes.

The fire started as a small, petrol-driven spot, but soon it burned high into the dark evening sky, the guy burning with it. We watched thousands of tiny orange embers lift high into the blackness.

As more adults arrived, rockets and roman candles lit up the night. Catherine wheels on Jim Murray's Dad's garden fence posts.

Soon the bonfire collapsed, tumbling in on itself, the heat coalescing in a central, churning, orange mass. I remember sometimes putting potatoes in the fire to roast, but can't recall ever eating them.

Then, when we were left with just the bonfire core.

We sat, unwilling to be dragged indoors until the fire was out. After all, it was our fire, and we'd worked hard for it.

But there was usually school the next day, and we were all called inside.

There was only one thought as we closed our eyes that night, dreaming of life's next milestone…

Christmas lay just round the corner!

2 Student Teachers, 5 Years Apart

Stobhill Primary. Maybe primary 5 (aged 10).

We got a guy as a student teacher that was older than our teacher (and that took some doing). He was nervous at first, but he soon opened up. Turns out he was ex RAF, and that meant he'd talk all day about flying warplanes.

The girls would go "really?" We didn't care.

He told us of flying, of Airplanes, of Spitfires and Hurricanes.

The boys sat rapt.

But times change… we got another student teacher…

Greenhall High school, second/third year, (aged maybe 14-15).

We got an actual French Student Teacher.

From France.

She had auburn hair, wore tight jeans and tight sweaters. As far as I can remember (and it was a while ago) she was called Mademoiselle Plasolles. She was SEX on a stick, and filled her jeans way better than the girls in our class. We'd sit with our tongues hanging out and on the ground. If she said the alphabet, we'd laugh. She was drop-down gorgeous. And she smelled. She smelled of stale tobacco and stale sweat. (Well, she *was* French) She was so good looking, it didn't make a difference to us. She would just sit and tell us stories of France.

The girls still said "really?" We still didn't care.

Moral of the story;

The actual objects of Boys interests change, but our passion does not.

High School Chemistry 1: Smells & Odours

Pear Drops

High School was a grand affair for us.
Budding Chemists.
The older we got, the more the teachers trusted us.
(Dumb, I know)
They let us go unescorted into the chemistry cupboard.
(Even dumber.)
We stole beakers, clamps, and test-tubes by the million. We took chemicals (wrapped in anything we could find) for our own experiments out-of-school, and literally left the place a virtual ghost town.

We also discovered Amyl Acetate, Pentyl Acetate, and Iso Amyl Acetate.

We knew it as the 'pear drop' smell. Like the boiled sweets we liked so much. I mean, if it smelled like sweets, it HAD to be alright.

Right?

We sniffed it like it was going out of fashion EVERY time we went into the cupboard. And that could be four, five times a lesson.

Now, again before you all go raising the roof, saying we were sniffing glue, please remember....

It was not glue. This stuff had NO adhesive qualities at all.

We were not sniffing it; we just liked the smell. NOT the same thing!

And how could it be wrong, when we knew the chemical formula.... We were students, for goodness sake.

And back in 1975, there was no problem with smelling this stuff. It was just a NICE SMELL.

Looking back, I always remember feeling kinda good after a few trips to the Chemistry Cupboard.

Only years later did I realize why. Woops.

Anyway.

Stink Bombs

Everyone does them. Bad egg smell.

Whatever.

When I was twelve I got a Chemistry set for Christmas one year and remember sitting behind the couch as Mum and Dad watched TV.

"Put Iron filings into beaker." My book said. So I did.

"Go to the cupboard and get some vinegar, pour over Iron filings." I did.

"In a while you will detect a bad smell. This is Hydrogen Sulfide."

"Bad Egg Gas."

Mum and Dad soon went daft.

I was banned from Chemistry indoors after that.

I protested innocently that it was in the book!

It had been in the Christmas present they'd given me!

Well, in High School, we did stink bombs, you know, a bit of iron filings, substitute Sulfuric Acid instead of household vinegar. The usual.

Then we got 'crafty'.

Mister Allen, our Chemistry teacher was getting wise to us, and we had to think outside the box, as it were.

Number one, Iron filings were passé, we needed something better to base it on, and I soon found it in the Chemistry Cupboard; Ferrous Sulfide.

Better concentration of Sulfur; much better.

We'd make 'time bombs'.

We'd suspend Ferrous Sulfide on paper, over a beaker of Sulfuric acid. But we'd soaked the paper in dilute acid, so it would give way about an hour later, leaving us free and dry on the blame game.

Too easy.

High School Chemistry 2: Gunpowder (Keeping the Legacy)

Pud and the Gunpowder

Well, we were soon sixteen; Fourth Years, just signed up for a fifth.

The elite.

And we all did Chemistry. And Physics.

A powerful mixture. And we lorded it over the serfs that we had been four years before.

We had leaders in the group, but that changed by the week. Whoever had the best experiment going.

George Learmonth was one such man. There's something about Scotland, that makes every 'George' into 'Pud' at school, and I have no idea why.

But George Learmonth was simply called Pud, to his friends.

He was a remnant from the year above, he had a motorbike; a green Honda CB125, and knew chemistry.

Man, did he know chemistry.

One day, he produced this photocopy of a book, he'd seen in the library. With a nervous look from one side to the other, he said we should make gunpowder.

And we, all being bright articulate students of the art of the chemical formula, instantly agreed.

Plus, it had to lead to us blowing stuff up. I mean, the word; gunpowder, kind of explained it all.

Now, I know what you all are going to say; "The recipe's on the internet!"

Ok, hot-shots, this was back in 1975. No internet.

Only by research did we come across this information... and the 'research' somehow made it legitimate.

"We need Fertilizer," Pud said. "And a whole lot of carbon."

Our Dads were all gardeners of some description, and all had some kind of fertilizer for their gardens. Whether the dads were growing prize winning roses, or the best vegetables, they needed fertilizer.

But we were students. Chemistry Students. We checked the chemical formulae on the packets for the right mix of Potassium and Ammonium Nitrate.

In the right mix, they'd make the biggest boom ever.

(Now again, you have to remember that this was way before terrorists would use the same mixes to do nefarious things to government buildings... this was different; we were chemists)

Ammonium Nitrate was the key ingredient, and we read all about it. In its most pure form, it made up the base for Nitroglycerin.

We were on a roll.

Carbon for the mix was also no problem. We all had coal fires in our houses, and the chimneys were swept regularly. Every garden had its 'soot pile'.

We raided our mum's cupboards for cups of sugar, it was a military operation. Then we mixed it with the soot.

Pure carbon, in both powder and crystalline form.

We tried it in small batches in secret trials. It hissed like gunpowder should, and gave off great clouds of dark, billowing smoke.

It was fantastic.

Over the weeks we refined the proportions.

Once it was perfect, we took packets of the stuff up the back field, dragged a ten yard trail (just like on TV) and watched it hiss then explode.

It took years for the grass to grow back.

Our batches got bigger and bigger.

Then we took a sack of it (A SACK!) up the Roman camp, a large area of waste ground and woodland. We found an anthill, dug a hole, and we poured it in. We were very safety conscious, and stood well back, then lit the dark, black trail.

It hissed, and burned, and hissed and burned. Then when it got to the anthill, it EXPLODED!

It sent earth and debris twenty, thirty, maybe fifty feet into the air.

This had an earthy, bass, boom. The ground shook beneath our feet. It had the dirt going everywhere; the whole nine yards.

Well back, we were very impressed. Not to mention a bit scared, because people from miles around would have seen the explosion.

We scattered in all directions, and never made gunpowder again.

Not because we were good, upstanding members of society.

But, because digging deep in the library, Pud had found something better.

Stealth Gunpowder

Now you can say what you like, I'm not a right-wing anarchist loony.

Whatever.

I'm NOT giving out this formula.

It involved a natural compound of Aluminium, (Aluminum to the US readers) and when crushed, was mixed with an acid to make a brown suspension, which was totally stable.

Now I repeat.

IT WAS TOTALLY STABLE.

When wet.

Now, I want to pause for a long time here for dramatic effect, but I can't do that, because of the medium I'm using, so please just assume there's a pause here.

For dramatic effect.

Anyway.

When we took this watery brown Aluminum compound suspension, and painted it on a door handle, for example, when it was wet it was stable.

When it was drying, it was stable.

But when it had actually dried, it became what's known in the scientific world as "Volatile".

The first bit of friction (like a hand grabbing the handle, for instance) and it went BANG!

No residue. No smoke. No flames. No trail leading back to us.

Just BANG!

We went wild; we painted handles until the teachers were frightened to open a door. We did chairs. We did window catches. We painted it on desks so when you opened it, nothing, but when you closed it…

BANG!

We laid puddles under the teacher's chairs, just waiting on them sitting down.

We went round the village, painting it on door knockers, and shop handles. But, that soon got boring.

So, to put some 'edge' back into it, we decided to go for the mother lode, and we made the biggest batch ever.

Now, before I continue, you have to remember here, that this was a more sophisticated level of explosive, and our father's sheds didn't have the basic materials…

All of the material for the 'stealth gunpowder' had to be 'borrowed' from the chemistry lab.

Only now, in bulk.

One lunchtime, we did without food, and painted the whole school front step, a HUGE step, right where the teachers would return from lunch.

We all waited in the bushes.

Seemingly forever.

I can't remember what teacher stepped on it, but the sound was out of this world.

There's not letters big enough to put on this page to describe the bang.

We lay low after that one.

Pud left school to join the Royal Air Force; perhaps the best place for him.

High School Chemistry: Purple Clouds and the Flood

The Purple and Yellow Cloud

There was another experiment worth mentioning, just because of the color.

Purple.

Purple's always interesting.

We learned that separate powders of Iodine and Magnesium were unstable in air. Mister Allen watched us that day, in our brand new small glass experiment room, attached to the main windows of the class.

The experiment was easy, and even looked kinda boring on paper.

Two tiny fragments of the substances, stand back.

Add water…. Purple and yellow smoke…… whatever.

It seemed so mundane.

But we did it.

Small granules, and using a pipette, a single drop of water on each, and…..

Absolutely gorgeous, distinctly separate plumes of deep purple and yellow smoke. They slowly wisped up into the air.

It truly was beautiful.

That purple cloud that resulted from the mix of smokes was so cute!

Real purple too. Not a hint, not a shade. Real royal purple.

Well.

We learned that day, that there is a reason that the textbooks direct you to use small quantities in experiments.

But we were pioneers….. so we took a handful of powders.

Well, not quite a handful, but certainly quite a bit more than the book directed.

And a cup of water.

94

And it took off like a volcano.

YELLOW! PURPLE!

But of course, we forgot, that a lot of purple smoke would soon be a HUGE purple cloud. Rapidly filling our room.

It wasn't the wispy cloud from before.

This was DEEP, we couldn't see anything, so we got to get the freak out of here.

PURPLE!

So we did what any chemistry student would have done...

We all left the room and shut the new air-tight door.

But we'd left in such a hurry, we still had not thought the whole thing through. The outside windows were closed!

That whole room went PURPLE... and stayed purple.

If you had been inside, you would not see your fingers if you stuck them IN your eye.

Mister Allen came into the department.

Took one look and told us to get in and open a window.

I still can't remember how we decided, but I know we drew lots, and Davie Hogg got the short straw.

With Mister Allen beside us, we opened the door, and Davie ran into a TOTALLY TOXIC, POISONOUS atmosphere.

And we shut the door after him!

Try telling that to the kids today!

In ten seconds flat, his hands appeared on the window of the door, and we let him out, along with the billowing purple cloud.

"Did you get it open?" we asked.

He coughed and spluttered, nodding furiously.

Basically, in the dark, the hero actually had made it past the experiment table, got to the window, opened it, and got back to the door.

Like true professionals, we decided that we would let loose this experiment on an unsuspecting Gorebridge.

We tried to get it home, but the powder was SO unstable.

Davey Hogg put a test-tube in the flap of his Adidas bag (we all had one, shut up!) sitting vertically, in case it leaked. Well, there must have been moisture in the tube, because it went off in class!

It shot a rocket of brown stuff into the air, shooting a hole in the ceiling tile.

Purple and yellow smoke was everywhere!

Luckily Mister Allen was out of the class at the time, and once the room was aired out, we sat for a very, sweaty, long 20 mins till the end of the period.

Right below the smashed ceiling tile.

Whew!

And you look at the modern Chemistry classroom of today. All, the safety goggles, white coats, crappy, non dangerous experiments.

I mean.

It never did us any harm.

Did it!

The Flood

There was one more incident worth telling, though it had little to do with Chemistry, it just started in that department.

We were standing in the small corridor outside Mister Allen's class, waiting to get in. Someone (may have been me, but I've never admitted it until now) playfully pushed Jock Devlin against the wall, and his heel hit the water main.

It went off like a snapped fire hydrant.

Water went everywhere.

We were quickly admitted to the classroom and Mister Allen rushed to get the janitor. But we were on the third floor, and the janitor was half a school away.

Well, us mischievous devils were left with a growing water problem, running in the open door to the chemistry lab.

What could we possibly do to help the problem?

(Help? Surely I meant alleviate?)

Not us!

We quickly grabbed every Bunsen burner we could find, (they always had a two foot tail of rubber tubing) and hooked them up to the water taps near the window, adding many more gallons to the impending flood. Bunsen burners were never designed to shoot water. It looked surreal.

Well, fun like that only lasts so long, and when the janitor arrived we were soon ushered out of the now totally waterlogged classroom, down to the next floor.

(We had replaced the Bunsen burners at the oncoming of teachers… we had people watching the stairs.)

The next floor down was the Art Department.

We looked up at the dripping ceiling tiles, and looked at the lights.

Quickly drawing for the honor, one of us switched them on.

BANG! BANG! BANG! All the way down the corridor.

(Kind of goes without saying, doesn't it)

Bright flash. Big Bang. No lights.

Ah, the good old days.

And try telling that to the youngsters of today. They'd never believe you.

And thus my memories fade. Thank you for reading.

As an author, I'd be delighted to have your thoughts on what you've just read. Your views on my writing style, the content, the storyline.

Even some memories of your own.

Good or bad, I'd like to hear from you.

Email me at; KansasScot@aol.com

Thank you.

And if you liked my writing, perhaps you'd go to wherever you bought this, and take a look at the other stuff I've written;

Scottish Adventure…

Vampire…

Self Help…

Printed in Great Britain
by Amazon